Vocation

God Serves through Us

The Lutheran Spirituality Series

Chad E. Hoover

Contents

Hymnal Key

LSB=Lutheran Service Book
ELH=Evangelical Lutheran Hymnary
CW=Christian Worship
LW=Lutheran Worship
LBW=Lutheran Book of Worship
TLH=The Lutheran Hymnal

About This Series

In the West, spirituality is as nebulous as it is popular. Having succumbed to humanism, rationalism, and Darwinism, communities once known for a genuine Christian piety now provide a fertile breeding ground for self-made theologies, Eastern religions, the worship of science and technology, or even a resuscitation of the old pagan gods. In a highly competitive environment, each of these spiritual philosophies seeks to fill the vacuum left by the seemingly departed Christian spirit.

Even among faithful Christians, and at other times and places, spirituality has run the gamut from the mystical to the almost sterile. From the emotional to the pragmatic, the experiential to the cerebral, the all-too-human desire to experience (and control!) the divine has proven to be especially resilient. Influenced by modernism, postmodernism, and whatever comes next, even those who try faithfully to follow Jesus Christ may find defining *spirituality*, or at least what is distinctively Christian about their own beliefs and practices, a significant challenge.

Do Lutheran Christians have a spirituality? Indeed they do! This adult Bible study series explores the rich depths of a distinctively Lutheran spirituality that begins in Baptism and is founded upon God's Word. There, the incarnate, crucified, and resurrected Lord proclaims His victory over sin, death, and the devil, and from there flows the proclamation of His Gospel and the administration of His Sacraments. It is through these means presented within the liturgy of His Church that Christ communicates not merely spiritual energies, an emotional high, a method of reasoning, or a stringent morality, but truly Himself—God in human flesh.

Written by respected Lutheran scholars in the United States and Australia, this adult Bible study series emphasizes the Bible, Luther's catechism, and the Lutheran hymnal as concrete and integral resources for a truly Lutheran spirituality. May God richly bless those who study His Word, and through His Word may they experience the genuinely enlightening and life-giving spirituality found only in the life, death, and resurrection of our Lord and Savior, Jesus Christ.

The Editor

Participant Introduction

In making conversation with a new acquaintance, one of the first questions we tend to ask is, "What do you do?" We'd be surprised if someone answered, "Well, I do a lot of things. I sing in the shower. I eat sushi. I mow my lawn every Saturday. And I watch a lot of TV." That's not the kind of answer we'd be looking for. What we really meant to ask was, "What do you do for a living? What is your job?"

We tend to think that, in large part, a person's *job* defines who that person *is*. In describing ourselves, we might even say, "I am an auto mechanic." "I am an engineer." "I am a teacher." Those who do not get paid for their work, such as homemakers, full-time students, or retirees, may feel out of sync with such an approach. Why? Because a person's job serves as an indication of his or her status in the world.

Vocation, however, includes more than just one's occupation. According to an individual's many callings in life, a person may be a husband or a wife, a father or a mother, a son or a daughter, a friend, a neighbor, a citizen, an employer, a mentor, or a volunteer in the community. The list goes on and on.

Scripture and the Lutheran Confessions proclaim and teach the true meaning of vocation. As children of God, we not only have a place in God's heavenly kingdom, but we also have been given a new status here in God's earthly kingdom. How do we balance this dichotomy?

Christians are faced with many questions about living a Christian life in a secular world: How can I live a Christian life in a secular workplace? Is my job, which is not directly affiliated with the Church, God-pleasing? How can I balance my calling as a Christian with my calling as a citizen of this community?

This study will examine these questions from a distinctly Lutheran perspective. The richness of the Gospel will be extolled as we explore this doctrine of vocation—a Christian's service to others and their service to us in this world.

To prepare for "God's Gifts through Vocation," read Luke 12:22–34.

ℭℬ

God's Gifts through Vocation

I believe that God has made me and all creatures; that He has given me my body and soul, eyes, ears, and all my members, my reason and all my senses, and still takes care of them. He also gives me clothing and shoes, food and drink, house and home, wife and children, land, animals, and all I have. He richly and daily provides me with all that I need to support this body and life. He defends me against all danger and guards and protects me from all evil. All this He does only out of fatherly, divine goodness and mercy, without any merit or worthiness in me. For all this it is my duty to thank and praise, serve and obey Him. This is most certainly true.

Martin Luther, explanation of the First Article
of the Apostles' Creed in the Small Catechism

In the late 1980s, the world was instructed in the philosophical wisdom of Bobby McFerrin with his catchy little tune "Don't Worry, Be Happy." In it, McFerrin warns against worry because when we do, we "make it double." In contrast, Jesus instructed His disciples, "Do not be anxious about your life, what you will eat, nor about your body, what you will put on" (Luke 12:22).

1. What is the difference between McFerrin's carefree, "Don't Worry, Be Happy" attitude to life and Jesus' words of consolation to His disciples?

God Provides All That Is Needful

2. Read Luke 12:23–28. How does Jesus show that God provides for all of His creation? What special place in this world has God given to human beings compared to the birds or the flowers in the fields?

3. How do we know—especially in the midst of sickness, suffering, and death—that God will provide for our daily needs?

4. How does Luther's explanation of the First Article of the Creed, quoted above, relate to the Fourth Petition of the Lord's Prayer, "Give us this day our daily bread"?

5. Discuss some of the many ways that God provides for our daily bread. Through whom does He provide it?

6. Read Luke 12:29–34. What gift is even more important than God's provision of clothing, food, and drink? How does knowing this help us to keep things in perspective when we believe we are in want?

7. List some of the differences between the ways that believers and unbelievers consider their temporal goods.

God's Gifts to You and through You

What else is all our work to God—whether in the fields, in the garden, in the city, in the house, in war, or in government—but [means] by which He wants to give His gifts in the fields, at home, and everywhere else? These are the masks of God, behind which He wants to remain concealed and do all things. . . . We have the saying: "God gives every good thing, but not just by waving a wand." God gives all good gifts; but you must lend a hand and take the bull by the horns; that is, you must work and thus give God good cause and a mask.

Martin Luther, AE 14:114–15

8. Luther described the various occupational roles—parents, farmers, laborers, soldiers, judges, retailers, and the like—as being "masks of God" (*larvae Dei*). Discuss how God has served you and continues to serve you behind the "masks" of other people. Give concrete examples.

9. Discuss how God is actively serving others through the vocations you have been given.

Gospel Character of Vocation

The doctrine of vocation is a great comfort for the Christian. Although vocation is an exercise of God's Law, it is very much driven and enabled by the Gospel. Because of sin, we all fail in our vocations, but God is continually with us, offering us the forgiveness of sins through Christ. He serves others through us despite our failures. Ultimately, we cannot take credit for the good works that we do because they are God's work.

10. Read John 15:5. Why is it not possible to do anything good apart from Christ (see also Romans 14:23; Ephesians 2:1)? How does your relationship with Christ affect your relationship with others?

11. How might God be serving others through you, perhaps even without your knowledge or despite your imperfections and sinfulness?

Spiritual Exercises

- This week, write on a sheet of paper the many ways that God is serving you through the vocations of others. Meditate on Psalm 145, praying portions of it each day and thanking God for each of these gracious provisions.
- Take time to examine yourself, identifying your many vocations and relationships with others, as Luther teaches in the section on Confession in the Small Catechism: "Consider your place in life according to the Ten Commandments: Are you a father, mother, son, daughter, husband, wife, or worker? Have you been disobedient, unfaithful, or lazy? Have you been hot-tempered, rude, or quarrelsome? Have you hurt someone by your words or deeds? Have you stolen, been negligent, wasted anything, or done any harm?" Confess your sins privately to

God; to your neighbor, if you have harmed him or her; or if your conscience is troubling you greatly, confess to your pastor, and receive the forgiveness of Christ.
• Reflecting upon what you've learned in this lesson, read Matthew 6:1–34. Study the section on the Lord's Prayer in Luther's Small Catechism.

Point to Remember

Your Father knows what you need before you ask Him. Matthew 6:8

To prepare for "Faith, Love, and the Christian Life," read 1 Thessalonians 1:1–10.

Faith, Love, and the Christian Life

*Therefore faith always justifies and makes alive; and yet it
does not remain alone, that is, idle. Not that it does not remain alone on its own level and in its own function, for it
always justifies alone. But it is incarnate and becomes man;
that is, it neither is nor remains idle or without love. Thus
Christ, according to His divinity, is a divine and eternal es-
sence or nature, without a beginning; but His humanity is a
nature created in time. These two natures in Christ are not
confused or mixed, and the properties of each must be clearly
understood. . . . Just as I am obliged to distinguish between
the humanity and the divinity, and to say: "The humanity
is not the divinity, and yet the man is God," so I make a distinction here and say: "The Law is not faith, and yet faith
does works. Faith and works are in agreement concretely or
compositely, and yet each has and preserves its own nature
and proper function."*

Martin Luther, AE 26:272–73

In his first epistle to the Thessalonians, Paul commended these
new Christians for their "work of faith and labor of love," which
served as "an example to all the believers in Macedonia and in
Achaia" (1 Thessalonians 1:3, 7). So, too, our union with Christ is
made evident by "faith working through love" (Galatians 5:6). A
proper view of the nature and role of faith and love in the Christian
life is necessary to understand the doctrine of vocation.

12. In what ways are *faith* and *love* understood in our society today?

Faith Working through Love

13. Read Genesis 12:1–4. Apart from God's promise, was there any reason why Abram should have believed that he would become the father of a great nation? What did his faith mean in regard to his status before the Lord (see Romans 4:1–5)?

14. Read Galatians 3:1–9, 14. How did the Galatians receive their faith? What did that mean for their Christian living?

15. Read Hebrews 11:8–12, 17–19. How did Abraham's faith express itself? Was Abraham righteous because of his works or because of his faith?

16. Read James 2:14–26. What naturally flows from a heart of faith, according to this passage?

17. Read John 15:1–8. Which comes first, bearing fruit for God or being united to Christ?

18. Read Matthew 25:31–46. In this analogy, how did the faith of the sheep express itself? How did the unbelief of the goats express itself?

The Place of Good Works in the Christian Life

"It is God's will, order, and command that believers should walk in good works. . . . Truly good works are done not by our own natural powers, but in this way: when a person is reconciled with God through faith and renewed by the Holy Spirit" (Formula of Concord, Solid Declaration IV 7). Further, Paul writes that a person is "created in Christ Jesus for good works" (Ephesians 2:10).

19. According to the Formula of Concord, why are our works as believing Christians pleasing to God but an unbeliever's works are not? What's the difference?

20. Are good works necessary in this life? What must happen first before a person can do anything good?

Living the Faith

James writes, "If a brother or sister is poorly clothed and lacking in daily food, and one of you says to them, 'Go in peace, be warmed and filled,' without giving them the things needed for the body, what good is that? So also faith by itself, if it does not have works, is dead" (James 2:15–17).

21. What are some ways that you can live out your faith in your community? How can your service to others be a witness to the love and mercy of Christ?

22. Read Ephesians 4:1–16. Although as redeemed children of God, we desire to do all things to the praise and glory of His name, what obstacles do we encounter as we attempt to live the faith? How does the Christian community support us?

Spiritual Exercises

- This week, review Luther's explanations to commandments Four through Ten. Note especially how he presents both the prohibitions ("You shall not") and the prescriptions ("You shall") in each commandment. For example, not only do we not murder our neighbor (the Fifth Commandment), we also "help and support him in every physical need."

- Use the hymn "I Know My Faith Is Founded" (*LSB* 587; *ELH* 494; *CW* 403; *LW* 354; *TLH* 381) for meditation in your daily devotions throughout the week. Focus especially on these words of the second stanza:

    Increase my faith, dear Savior, For Satan seeks by night and day To rob me of this treasure And take my hope of bliss away. But, Lord, with You beside me, I shall be undismayed; And led by Your good Spirit, I shall be unafraid. Abide with me, O Savior, A firmer faith bestow; Then I shall bid defiance To ev'ry evil foe.

- Read 1 Corinthians 13:4–8a. First, note how you can express your faith in love to others in the ways described in this passage. Second, rejoice that God expresses His love and service to you in a similar manner through Jesus Christ, His Son.

Point to Remember

Truly, I say to you, as you did it to one of the least of these My brothers, you did it to Me. Matthew 25:40

To prepare for "Spiritual Living in an Unspiritual Word," read Ephesians 2:1–22.

Ↄↄ

Spiritual Living in an Unspiritual World

Thus a Christian man who lives in this confidence toward God knows all things, can do all things, ventures everything that needs to be done, and does everything gladly and willingly, not that he may gather merits and good works, but because it is a pleasure for him to please God in doing these things. He simply serves God with no thought of reward, content that his service pleases God. On the other hand, he who is not at one with God, or is in a state of doubt, worries and starts looking about for ways and means to do enough and to influence God with his many good works. He runs off to St. James, to Rome, to Jerusalem, hither and thither; he prays St. Bridget's prayer, this prayer and that prayer; he fasts on this day and that day; he makes confession here and makes confession there; he questions this man and that man, and yet finds no peace. He does all this with great effort and with a doubting and unwilling heart, so that the Scriptures rightly call such works . . . labor and sorrow. And even then they are not good works and are in vain.

Martin Luther, AE 44:27

How are Christians different from everyone else? Our world, and even some Christian denominations, see Christianity basically as a religion of morality. In other words, some Christians strive to live under the Law of God, seeking to earn His favor. This is impossible. On the other hand, some Christians think that good works are not at all necessary in the Christian life. This is a mistake as well.

23. Can we really recognize genuine Christians, based on works alone, within our community? Do good works alone make someone a Christian?

In the World, But Not of the World

24. Read John 17:11–26. In His High Priestly Prayer, what does Jesus say about a Christian's relationship to the world? If the world is so bad, why doesn't Jesus pray for His disciples to be taken out of it?

25. How does Jesus preserve believers in a world that hates them? What is Christ's desire for all believers?

26. Read Ephesians 2:1–9. Despite this broken relationship between God and humanity due to humanity's sin, what place do believers have in God's heavenly kingdom? How is this possible?

27. Read Romans 12:1–2, 17–21, and Ephesians 2:10. Having been redeemed by God through the shedding of Christ's blood on the cross, what are Christians called to do in this world?

28. Read Romans 13:1–7 and 1 Peter 2:13–25. How do Christians relate to earthly authorities? For what purpose do earthly governments serve?

29. Read John 18:33–38 and 19:9–12. How does Jesus distinguish God's kingdom of grace from God's kingdom of earthly government?

Living in Two Kingdoms

For the Christian, a proper distinction between God's earthly governance and His heavenly governance must be maintained. God rules and reigns over both kingdoms, but He does so in different ways. As part of God's creation, we hold citizenship in His earthly kingdom and are subject to God's Law. As God's new creation in Christ, we are subjects under God's Gospel and hold citizenship in His heavenly kingdom as well.

30. How does God deal with you as a part of His creation, according to the standards of His earthly kingdom? How does God deal with you as a new creation in Christ, according to the standards of His heavenly kingdom?

31. What are some examples of how these two kingdoms might be confused, and what is the danger in doing so?

Will This World Ever Change?

Thirty years ago, a famous Coca-Cola jingle suggested that the world could sing in "perfect harmony." This message of peace struck such a chord that the song became a pop hit when it was recorded as a single in 1971. Although well-intentioned, the aspiration to reach "perfect harmony" in this present, fallen world is both unrealistic and a denial of sin. People keep expecting that this world will change, but will it?

32. In the past thirty years, has the world gotten any closer to "perfect harmony"? What about in the past five? Why or why not?

33. Read 2 Corinthians 4:8–18. How is a Christian to react to the ceaseless sinfulness and hostility of the world?

Spiritual Exercises

• Use the service of Morning Prayer (*LSB*, pp. 235–42) as your morning devotion. Note how this service ascribes praise to God both as our Savior and as the provider of our daily needs.

• Christ serves us in His Word and Sacraments. Review commandments One through Three and their explanations in Luther's Small Catechism, giving thanks to God—Father, Son, and Holy Spirit—for His precious name and His holy Word.

• Also review the Fourth Commandment and its explanation in Luther's Small Catechism. Note that the authority God gives to fathers and mothers also extends to all earthly authorities. Pray that the Holy Spirit would guide you to identify any sin in your life so that you may repent of it, receive forgiveness, and strive to obey all those that God has placed in authority over you.

Point to Remember

For by grace you have been saved through faith. And this is not your own doing; it is the gift of God, not a result of works, so that no one may boast. For we are His workmanship, created in Christ Jesus for good works, which God prepared beforehand, that we should walk in them. Ephesians 2:8–10

To prepare for "Vocation in the Christian Home," read Ephesians 5:21–6:4.

Vocation in the Christian Home

When I have this righteousness within me, I descend from heaven like the rain that makes the earth fertile. That is, I come forth into another kingdom, and I perform good works whenever the opportunity arises. . . . If I am a father, I rule my household and family, I train my children in piety and honesty. . . . In short, whoever knows for sure that Christ is his righteousness not only cheerfully and gladly works in his calling but also submits himself . . . to everything else in this present life—even, if need be, to burden and danger. For he knows that God wants this and that this obedience pleases Him. . . .

The Spirit is whatever is done in us through the Spirit; the flesh is whatever is done in us in accordance with the flesh and apart from the Spirit. Therefore all the duties of Christians—such as loving one's wife, rearing one's children, governing one's family, honoring one's parents, obeying the magistrate, etc., . . .—are fruits of the Spirit.

Martin Luther, AE 26:11–12, 217

A child's first teachers are his or her parents. However, many parents today feel ill-equipped to teach their children about the Christian faith. Sadly, it appears that even some Christian churches are incapable of aiding parents in this task.

34. How has the transmission of the Christian faith within families fared over the past fifty years? the past twenty? ten? Is there a rela-

tionship between these changes and the overall decline in religious beliefs and values in our culture?

God-Given Roles within the Home

35. Read Genesis 1:27–28 and 2:18–25. A new vocation arises within the Christian home when God joins a man and a woman together in marriage. What are the purposes for marriage, according to these passages?

36. Read Ephesians 5:21–33. What additional duties do husbands and wives have according to Paul? How do his directives help to produce a smooth and harmonious home? What difficulties do married couples encounter when attempting to adhere to Paul's instructions?

37. How does human marriage between a husband and a wife illustrate Christ's relationship with His bride, the Church? What significance does this place upon one's vocation within marriage?

38. Read Ephesians 6:1–4. Vocation within the home expands when children are brought into the marriage. What new duties do husbands and wives have when they become parents?

39. What is God's calling for children, and what is their role within the home? Why should fathers in particular not anger their children?

40. Read Psalm 127. What special status does God give children within the family? What does the psalmist say is a necessary foundation for raising faithful children? Why is this true?

Treasuring Catechesis

"Train up a child in the way he should go; even when he is old he will not depart from it" (Proverbs 22:6). Parents have a God-given duty to instruct their children in the faith. That is why many of the Six Chief Parts in Luther's Small Catechism begins with the phrase "As the head of the family should teach it in a simple way to his household."

41. Discuss the benefits of using Luther's Small Catechism at home to teach the Christian faith to children. How might parents also be blessed in doing this?

42. What is the relationship between the education parents give their children in the home and the education children receive in Sunday School, confirmation class, or a Lutheran Day School?

Distinction between Office and Person

"To the position of fatherhood and motherhood God has given special distinction above all positions that are beneath it: He does not simply command us to love our parents, but to honor them. Regarding our brothers, sisters, and neighbors in general, He commands nothing more than that we love them [Matthew 22:39; 1 John 3:14]. In this way He separates and distinguishes father and mother from all other persons upon earth and places them at His side." (Large Catechism I 105)

43. Which do you consider to be more important: that children *like* their parents or that children *honor* their parents? Are both possible?

44. A father's authority over his household does not give him license to lord it over his wife and children. How can parents lovingly serve their children while maintaining the authority that God commands?

Spiritual Exercises

- If you do not do so already, have regular devotions with your spouse or family. (If you are single or an empty nester, consider inviting a relative, friend, co-worker, or neighbor to join you.) *The Lord Will Answer: A Daily Prayer Catechism* (CPH, 2004) is a good resource that takes you through each section of Luther's Small Catechism with short devotions for each day of the year.
- Pray the following hymns this week, noting how each extols the blessings God gives through spouse, family, children, and vocation:
  S. "Oh, Blest the House" (*LSB* 862; *ELH* 190; *CW*; 506; *LW* 467; *LBW* 512; *TLH* 625)
  M. "Our Father, by Whose Name" (*LSB* 863; *ELH* 187; *CW* 501; *LW* 465; *LBW* 357)
  T. "Lord, Help Us Ever to Retain" (*LSB* 865; *ELH* 551; *CW* 514; *LW* 477; *TLH* 288)
  W. "Lord Jesus Christ, the Children's Friend" (*LSB* 866; *CW*

513; *LW* 470)
T. "Let Children Hear the Mighty Deeds" (*LSB* 867; *ELH* 180; *CW* 512; *LW* 472; *TLH* 629)
F. "How Clear Is Our Vocation, Lord" (*LSB* 853)
S. "Lord, Help Us Walk Your Servant Way" (*LSB* 857)
•   Learn Ephesians 5:1–2 by heart.

Point to Remember

Unless the LORD builds the house, those who build it labor in vain. Psalm 127:1

To prepare for "Christianity in the Workplace," read Ephesians 6:5–9.

ભ

Christianity in the Workplace

*Therefore, if we recognize the great and precious things
which are given us, as Paul says [Rom. 5:5], our hearts will
be filled by the Holy Spirit with the love which makes us
free, joyful, almighty workers and conquerors over all tribu-
lations, servants of our neighbors, and yet lords of all. For
those who do not recognize the gifts bestowed upon them
through Christ, however, Christ has been born in vain; they
go their way with their works and shall never come to taste
or feel those things. Just as our neighbor is in need and lacks
that in which we abound, so we were in need before God and
lacked his mercy. Hence, as our heavenly Father has in
Christ freely come to our aid, we also ought freely to help our
neighbor through our body and its works, and each one
should become as it were a Christ to the other that we may
be Christs to one another and Christ may be the same in all,
that is, that we may be truly Christians.*

Martin Luther, AE 31:367–68

Christians are engaged in the culture, involved in the fabric of
society. That means Christians go to the movies, eat at local restau-
rants, and cheer on their favorite team at the ballpark. Christians also
hold a vast assortment of occupations. Maybe your hair dresser is a
Christian, or perhaps the pizza delivery person, or even the mayor.
Think about your own place of employment. Many workplaces have
Christians and non-Christians working side by side doing the same or
similar jobs.

45. Do you think there are certain occupations Christians

should never hold? Name some of them. Name any occupations you think non-Christians should not hold.

Relationships in the Workplace

46. Read Ephesians 6:5–8. Christians in the workplace may find themselves in positions of authority or in positions under authority. What directives does Paul give for those working under the authority of another?

47. Is it ever easy to wholeheartedly serve one's master or boss? Why or why not? What circumstances make it even more difficult?

48. Read Ephesians 6:9. How should those in authority act toward those working under them? In what way does the "master" have an even greater duty than the "servant"?

49. Paul notes that "there is no partiality" with God (see also Luke 1:51–53; Acts 10:34–35, 44–48; Galatians 3:26–29). For what purpose, then, do distinctions within earthly relationships serve?

50. Read Matthew 20:1–16. How is the kingdom of heaven like the master of the house hiring workers for his vineyard? How does

this parable, though it teaches a heavenly truth, represent poor business practice according to the world's standards?

51. Should a Christian employer adopt this sort of practice in running his or her business? What would happen if this model were put forward in the world?

Working in a Secular Environment

Living our Christian lives in the workplace begins with receiving Christ's gifts in the Divine Service. The Christian life is about *being* before it is about *doing*. We need the refreshment and encouragement that the Holy Spirit provides us through the Gospel and the Sacraments to strengthen us for the daily grind. In loving response to Christ's gifts, we serve God by serving our neighbors—including those we interact with at work.

52. What challenges might Christians face working in a predominantly non-Christian environment? How can these be overcome?

53. List some of the reasons why you go to church. Which is (are) the most important? How does Sunday worship refresh you for another work week?

Worship beyond the Sanctuary

Peter writes, "Always [be] prepared to make a defense to anyone who asks you for a reason for the hope that is in you; yet do it with gentleness and respect, having a good conscience, so that, when you are slandered, those who revile your good behavior in Christ may be put to shame" (1 Peter 3:15–16). Though applicable to many situations in life, Peter's words hold great significance for the workplace.

54. How does the workplace provide Christians with a unique, although sometimes very challenging, opportunity for evangelism?

55. What are some effective ways for a Christian to live the Christian life in the workplace?

Spiritual Exercises

- Take brief times out of your workday to pray for your co-workers, for your supervisor(s), or for those under your supervision. Pray that you would be faithful in your duties, rendering service to your neighbors in the workplace as you would to the Lord.
- As you rest from your labors this week, meditate upon Psalm 92 and rejoice in the labors of God's hands for His people. May this encouraging Word rejuvenate you as you enter into His harvest field each day.
- Review the Second Article of the Creed and its explanation in Luther's Small Catechism. Marvel at the work of Christ on our behalf. Trust not in your own work for salvation but only in the merits of our Lord.

Point to Remember

For you, O LORD, have made me glad by your work; at the works of your hands I sing for joy. Psalm 92:4

To prepare for "Freedom of the Christian," read Galatians 5:1–18.

CB

Freedom of the Christian

A Christian is a perfectly free lord of all, subject to none. A Christian is a perfectly dutiful servant of all, subject to all. These two theses seem to contradict each other. If, however, they should be found to fit together they would serve our purpose beautifully. Both are Paul's own statements, who says in 1 Cor. 9[:19], "For though I am free from all men, I have made myself a slave to all," and in Rom. 13[:8], "Owe no one anything, except to love one another." Love by its very nature is ready to serve and be subject to him who is loved. So Christ, although he was Lord of all, was "born of woman, born under the law" [Gal. 4:4], and therefore was at the same time a free man and a servant, "in the form of God" and "of a servant" [Phil. 2:6–7].

Martin Luther, AE 31:344

Luther points out the paradoxical nature of the Christian life: Christians are both lords and servants, freemen and slaves. Luther admits that these two ideas seem to contradict each other, but he assures us that both are based upon the clear teaching of Scripture.

56. Having Jesus by our side, are we free to do whatever we want, such as running red lights? Why or why not? How does the distinction of the two kingdoms help us understand the freedom we enjoy as Christians?

Slaves unto Righteousness

57. Read Galatians 5:1–6. From what has Christ freed us? Why is it detrimental to our faith to believe, even in part, that our salvation and our relationship with God is based upon our performance?

58. Read Galatians 5:13–15. Though Christians have been set free by Christ, what does this freedom *not* entail?

59. Read Galatians 5:16–18. The flesh, our corrupt sinful nature, fights against the Holy Spirit, who dwells within us. How does our twofold nature as sinner and saint affect the freedom we have in Christ?

60. Read 1 Corinthians 10:23–11:1. Christians have been set free by Christ, but under some circumstances they may choose not to exercise their freedom. What are such circumstances, and how is this willing service different from the yoke of slavery Paul speaks about in Galatians 5?

61. Read Romans 6:15–23. In one Epistle, Paul boldly asserts that Christians are freed by Christ. In another, he declares that Christians are slaves to righteousness. How is this possible?

62. How does the fact that we as Christians are slaves to righteousness shape our understanding of the doctrine of Christian vocation?

Freed to Serve

The forgiveness that Christ so freely gives has set us free to serve our neighbor. All concerns that we may have about our own salvation have been alleviated by the Words and work of our Savior, who for the joy that was set before Him endured the cross (Hebrews 12:2). Indeed, it is for freedom that Christ has set us free!

63. Read Matthew 18:21–35. How has Christ's forgiveness set us free from our sins? What has this forgiveness freed us to do?

64. How does the understanding of salvation as God forgiving our sins for Christ's sake not only generate our desire to evangelize but also give shape to our methods of evangelism?

The Reality of Sin

Good works are not necessary for salvation, but they are necessary (see Augsburg Confession VI; Apology of the Augsburg Confession XIIb 77). Though Christians daily battle the sinful flesh, we rejoice with Paul, who wrote, "I have been crucified with Christ. It is no longer I who live, but Christ who lives in me. And the life I now live in the flesh I live by faith in the Son of God, who loved me and gave himself for me" (Galatians 2:20).

65. Read Romans 7:14–25. What are some examples of how we Christians struggle to keep the Law? Should these struggles concern us?

66. Read Romans 8:1–4. Should we be concerned if we don't struggle against the sinful flesh? Why? How is Christ our only hope and the source not only of forgiveness of sins but also for living the Christian life?

Spiritual Exercises

- During the coming week, meditate each day on the hymn "Salvation unto Us Has Come" (*LSB* 555; *ELH* 227; *CW* 390; *LW* 355; *LBW* 297; *TLH* 377). Note how Law and Gospel are distinguished, how Christ's work for us is exalted, and how the fruit of good works is portrayed as evidence of a living faith.
- In consideration of Paul's words in 1 Corinthians 10:23–11:1, analyze your attitude and actions this past week to see if your exercise of your Christian freedom has caused offense to your neighbor. With the Holy Spirit's guidance, confess where you have sinned, and look for ways to serve that person in love. Rejoice that God has forgiven your sins for Christ's sake.
- If you have not already done so, commit to memory Luther's explanation of the Third Article of the Creed.

Point to Remember

But thanks be to God, that you who were once slaves of sin have become obedient from the heart to the standard of teaching to which you were committed, and, having been set free from sin, have become slaves of righteousness. Romans 6:17–18

Leader Guide

Leaders, please note the different abilities of your Bible study participants. Some will easily find the many passages listed in this study. Others will struggle to find even the "easy" passages. To help everyone participate, team up members of the class. For example, if a question asks you to look up several passages, assign one passage to one group, the second to another, and so on. Divide up the work! Let participants present the different answers they discover.

Each topic is divided into four easy-to-use sections.

Focus: introduces participants to key concepts that will be discovered in the session.

Inform: guides participants into Scripture to uncover truth concerning a doctrine.

Connect: enables participants to apply that which is learned in Scripture to their lives and provides them an opportunity to formulate and articulate a defense of a key doctrine.

Vision: provides participants with practical suggestions for extending the theme of the lesson out of the classroom and into the world.

God's Gifts through Vocation

Objectives

By the power of the Holy Spirit working through God's Word, participants will (1) recognize God's gifts to His creation through their own vocations and the vocations of others, (2) compare and contrast God's temporal gifts to God's eternal gifts, and (3) understand more clearly how God "richly and daily provides [them] with all that [they] need to support this body and life" (Luther's Small Catechism, explanation of the First Article of the Creed).

Opening Worship

Gracious Father, You have created this world by Your goodness and continue to sustain it through Your mighty power. Grant that we may be led by Your Holy Spirit to see and understand Your gracious work among us through vocation, so that we may be ever ready to serve others through the various gifts and talents that You have given to us; through Jesus Christ, Your Son, our Lord. Amen.

Sing "Praise to the Lord, the Almighty" (*LSB* 790; *ELH* 65; *CW* 234; *LW* 444; *LBW* 543; *TLH* 39).

Focus

1. Read or ask a participant to read the first paragraph aloud. In Luke 12:22, Jesus is not denying the presence of trouble in our world. He is not suggesting, like McFerrin's ditty, "Don't worry, because there's really nothing to worry about. If it weren't for all your worrying, everything would be fine." Rather, Jesus is saying, "Do not worry, because your Father knows what you need. Even in the midst of trouble (caused by sin in the world), God is in control and provides for you in this life."

God Provides All That Is Needful (Inform)

2. Human beings have been given a special place of authority over the rest of God's creation (see Genesis 1:26–28). In this passage

from Luke, Jesus illustrates the heavenly Father's care for humankind by showing His great care and provision for objects of lesser value (birds, flowers) within His creation. Jesus teaches us that we do not need to worry about the daily needs of this life because through His goodness and mercy, our heavenly Father provides for our needs in great abundance.

3. We can trust God only because we've been given faith. Apart from the gift of faith, we cannot believe that "life is more than food, and the body more than clothing." Despite our distressing circumstances, God's Word of promise sustains us. This is something that the world cannot give; only Christ gives us the strength to see through our hardships.

4. Discuss the First Article gifts—those that God gives through His creation—listed in Luther's explanation. God gives us all things that we need for this body and life, that is, "our daily bread." This confident belief in God's providential care is also reflected in Luther's explanation of the Fourth Petition of the Lord's Prayer.

5. God provides bread through the work of the grocer, who sells the bread to us. But before that, God provided flour for the baker, and before that, seed for the farmer. Assist participants in giving other examples. Though God could miraculously provide daily bread for His creation as He did for the Israelites in the wilderness (see Exodus 16), He chooses to meet our earthly needs through the vocations of others. God even uses unwilling, unknowing, or unbelieving servants to carry out His work. We may have an unbelieving doctor, attorney, or electrician, for example, who nevertheless performs his or her services for us and does them well.

6. More important than earthly clothing, food, or drink, God clothes believers with Christ and His righteousness (Galatians 3:27; Philippians 3:8–9) and grants them the forgiveness of sins and eternal life in His kingdom through faith in His name (Luke 24:46–47; John 3:16; Acts 2:38–39).

The First Article gifts that God gives us are here today but gone tomorrow. They are good gifts, but they are temporary. They wear out. They rot and decay. Faith, however, is the God-given gift (Ephesians 2:8–9) that apprehends Christ's saving work and that opens eternal life to all believers. God grants and strengthens this gift of faith through the Gospel and the Sacraments.

7. Ultimately, all good gifts are from God. Whether people realize it or not, God has blessed His entire creation with many gifts. Without God's sustenance, life on this earth would cease to exist.

Even though sinful humans do not always perfectly trust in God's provision for their needs, God does not cease to provide for His creation. His provision for the needs of body and life are not dependent upon faith. God "makes His sun rise on the evil and on the good, and sends rain on the just and on the unjust" (Matthew 5:45). In his explanation of the Fourth Petition of the Lord's Prayer, Luther writes, "God certainly gives daily bread to everyone without our prayers, even to all evil people, but we pray in this petition that God would lead us to realize this and to receive our daily bread with thanksgiving" (Luther's Small Catechism).

God's Gifts to You and through You (Connect)

8. Luther frequently used the term the *masks of God* (*larvae Dei*) to describe the means God uses to work on our behalf and to show Himself while remaining hidden. What does a mask do? It hides someone's face. If a person's vocation is a mask of God, then God is hidden but is still at work on our behalf. He is not seen in the work, but He is there nonetheless.

The purpose of our vocation is to serve our neighbor. Schoolwork, a daily nine-to-five job, or chores around the house can at times seem frustrating, pointless, and exhausting. However, as a new creation in Christ, our works have been sanctified; that is, they are continually made clean by His Holy Spirit. No matter how mundane or ordinary the work, it has meaning and significance because God is working through the believer's vocation for the benefit of his or her neighbor.

9. Answers will vary. Assist participants in discussing the concrete ways and the masks behind which God is serving them.

Gospel Character of Vocation (Vision)

10. Apart from Christ, we could do nothing because we were dead in our trespasses and sins. Anything that does not proceed from faith is sin (Romans 14:23). Our union with Christ gives us everything! He has freed us from the bondage of our sin, and He gives us the power to truly serve our neighbor and do good works. Furthermore, because God has promised to provide for our bodily needs, we are free to serve our neighbor without worry for ourselves.

11. Answers will vary depending upon the vocations represented in the group. At times, we may question our place in God's kingdom. Perhaps it seems that we're always letting God down. Maybe we ha-

ven't been a faithful witness or a humble servant in all areas of our lives. Thankfully, our relationship with Him is not dependent upon our works; it's dependent upon God and His promises to us in Christ. In terms of our salvation and our place in God's everlasting kingdom, we have a guarantee signed with the blood of Christ and sealed with the gift of the Holy Spirit (see Ephesians 1:7–14).

Often we are not even aware of the many ways in which God is working through us to serve our neighbor. At other times, we are all too aware, and vocation turns into a burden or a cross to bear. However, "You were washed, you were sanctified, you were justified in the name of the Lord Jesus Christ and by the Spirit of our God" (1 Corinthians 6:11). The Holy Spirit is continually at work in and through you. Your sanctification means that despite the sinfulness that is inseparable from your flesh, God purifies your works so that they have everlasting significance. Through faith in Christ, your love and work for your neighbor is truly a good work in God's sight.

Faith, Love, and the Christian Life

Objectives

By the power of the Holy Spirit working through God's Word, participants will (1) realize that faith works through love and that the Gospel inspires and enables a Christian's good works, (2) articulate the proper understanding of good works for the Christian, and (3) be equipped with examples of living the faith.

Opening Worship

Direct us, O Lord, in all our doings with Your most gracious favor, and further us with Your continual help that in all our works begun, continued, and ended in You we may glorify Your holy name and finally by Your mercy obtain eternal salvation; through Jesus Christ, our Lord. Amen.

Sing "Take My Life and Let It Be" (*LSB* 783; *ELH* 444; *CW* 469; *LW* 404; *LBW* 406; *TLH* 400).

Focus

12. In our world, the word *faith* is typically defined as confidence in oneself, in another person or group, or in a particular outcome. For example, "I have faith in you, Jimmy! You can beat that nasty habit." The word *love* is used flippantly in our culture: "I love sports!" "I love cookies!" "I loved that movie!" "I love you, man!" Lead participants in a discussion about *faith* and *love* and how these two words are used in our society. Note the various connotations, nuances, and definitions of each.

Faith Working through Love (Inform)

13. There was nothing in Abram himself that would allow him to believe anything God was promising. Abram was childless. How could he be the father of a great nation if his wife could not even bear

38

a son? Abram did not choose God, but God chose him. Despite the incapacity of Abram's sinful flesh, God gave him faith to believe God's promise, and Abram's faith was credited to him as righteousness (see also Genesis 15:6; Romans 4:1–12; Hebrews 11:8–12, 17–19). The same gift of God-given faith in Christ as our Savior connects us with Christ and all other believers.

14. God gave the Galatians, and gives all believers, the gift of faith through hearing the Gospel, not by observing the works of the Law. Receiving the Holy Spirit and faith through the proclamation of the Gospel and through Holy Baptism is the beginning of the Christian life. Paul reminds the Galatians that the Christian life is not only begun in the Holy Spirit, but it continues day by day in God's grace. Works of the flesh, as Paul calls them, do not in any way bring a person into a closer relationship with God. However, the Gospel, which we have received through faith, both motivates and enables us to do good works, or acts of love for the benefit of our neighbor. For further discussion, assist participants in reviewing the Third Article of the Creed in Luther's Small Catechism.

15. Sadly, some Christians are taught that Old Testament believers were saved by their works, their keeping of the Law. However, that is not true. Like us, God saved them by His grace, through faith without works, although faith is always accompanied by good works. Faith precedes action in the Christian life. Note in Hebrews 11:8–12, 17–19 the number of things that Abraham did by faith. These things did not save him or cause God to declare him righteous. Rather, it was his faith that saved him and that resulted in good works.

16. In his Epistle, James uses the example of Abraham to illustrate how faith results in obedience to God. James does not deny the necessity of faith. The well-known saying is true: "We are saved by faith alone, but faith is never alone." James's message is God's Word, and it is consistent with the whole of Scripture. However, James reminds his readers that true faith is active in works. If good works are absent, then where is the faith? Is it dead? It would certainly appear so. Love for God and love for your neighbor naturally flow from a heart of faith.

17. Christians are made clean not because they bear fruit; they are made clean through the grace of God and the power of the Holy Spirit. Faith is a prerequisite for any and all good works. For apart from being connected to Christ (the Vine), we (the branches) cannot do anything. Christians abide in the love of Christ so we can serve our neighbor with that same love. Without Christ as a foundation,

our good works would wither away and die, just like a branch that has been cut off from a vine. The vine is the source of life for that branch. Without it, the branch cannot live.

18. The sheep (the righteous) did everything perfectly in the eyes of the Father. They fed the hungry, gave drink to the thirsty, welcomed the stranger, clothed the naked, and visited the sick and those in prison. Notice that Jesus never enumerates the sins of these who are on His right. Have they kept God's Law perfectly? No, they have not. But Christ has, and He has done it for them and for all people—thereby giving significance to these relatively menial acts of love and charity. Through faith, the sheep did indeed do good works.

On the other hand, the goats (the unrighteous) did not bear any fruit. Jesus says, point-blank, that they have not fed the hungry, given drink to the thirsty, welcomed the stranger, clothed the naked, or visited the sick and those in prison. But haven't they done anything good? Externally, it appears that they have. But the Father doesn't recognize these works because they have not proceeded from faith. Though unbelievers may reach out to others with seeming charity, without faith their works are sin (Romans 14:23).

The Place of Good Works in the Christian Life (Connect)

19. Although unbelievers do "civil works" (external works that appear to be good), without faith in the crucified and resurrected Savior, God does not consider them to be good works at all (see Apology of the Augsburg Confession V 9–10). Works done without faith are impure because they do not flow from regenerate hearts, that is, hearts that have been regenerated by God. On this point Scripture is clear: "For whatever does not proceed from faith is sin" (Romans 14:23). For further discussion about this point, the leader may suggest that participants read the Formula of Concord, Solid Declaration IV.

20. Good works are *not* necessary for salvation, but they *are* necessary (see Augsburg Confession VI; Apology of the Augsburg Confession V 1–4; Formula of Concord, Epitome IV, Solid Declaration IV). However, good works apart from Christ are not good works at all. Just as it is impossible for a banana tree to grow oranges, it is impossible to for an unbeliever to produce good works. If you want oranges, you need an orange tree. If you want to produce good works, you must be in Christ, who is the source of true goodness.

Living the Faith (Vision)

21. Answers will vary. Read 1 John 3:16–17, where John writes very explicitly of what love is, namely, Christ laying down His life for us on the cross. We show love in a similar way by our willingness to lay down our lives for our brothers and sisters. We may say, "I love you," but even more than mere words or feelings, our actions show others the love of Christ that abides in us.

22. Answers may vary. All obstacles that we face are part of the struggle of the Christian life. We will fail to do all things to the glory of God; this is unavoidable. The only reconciliation we have with God comes through the blood Christ shed upon the cross. God forgave our sins for Christ's sake, and through the Gospel and the Sacraments, God applies Christ's atonement and perfect life to us. We are cleansed and reconciled with God the Father. However, a Christian is not alone in this world. The Holy Spirit works through our pastors, teachers, congregation members, and Christian family and friends to encourage us in living the faith.

Spiritual Living in an Unspiritual World

Objectives

By the power of the Holy Spirit working through God's Word, participants will (1) recognize that Christians are in the world, but not of the world; (2) understand the distinction between God's earthly kingdom and His heavenly kingdom; and (3) affirm that this world is only temporary and that it will always be a sinful and hostile place until Christ returns.

Opening Worship

Almighty God, because You know that we are set among so many and great dangers that by reason of the weakness of our fallen nature we cannot always stand upright, grant us Your strength and protection to support us in all dangers and carry us through all temptations; through our Lord Jesus Christ, Your Son, who lives and reigns with You and the Holy Spirit, one God, now and forever. Amen.

Sing "A Mighty Fortress Is Our God" (*LSB* 656; *ELH* 250; *CW* 200; *LW* 297; *LBW* 228; *TLH* 262).

Focus

23. Read or ask a participant to read the opening paragraph. Christianity and morality are not synonymous. If they were, then there would be many unbelievers who are "better Christians" than many of us. Holding to a particular set of moral standards is not what makes a person a Christian. Rather, what makes someone a Christian is repentant faith in Jesus Christ. We would certainly expect Christians to live morally upright lives, have compassion for those in need, rally for worthwhile causes, and so on. However, it is not the works they do that actually make them Christians. These good works are the "fruits of faith," which ensue from a heart that has been regenerated by the Holy Spirit through the Gospel.

In the World, But Not of the World (Inform)

24. In His High Priestly Prayer, Jesus says that His disciples (and ultimately all Christians) will be hated by the world because they are not of the world, just as He is not of it. Jesus prays for His disciples to remain in the world, however, so that they can be sent into it with the Good News of Christ (v. 18). This apostolic word must be proclaimed so that the benefits of Christ's life, death, and resurrection will be spread throughout the world. Though we struggle in this sinful world, we remain in it for the sake of those who have not yet heard the Word of life. Faith comes through hearing the Word about Christ (see Romans 10:13–17).

25. Christ's mission is to redeem God's fallen creation and bring it back into a right relationship with Him. This is not done by means of the world, but only through Christ. Christ sanctifies Himself, that is, He dedicates Himself to this task of salvation so that we are cleansed of our sinfulness and accepted by God on account of Him. Christ's Word is truth, and it is the Holy Spirit working through this Word that sanctifies us.

Note: Sanctification can be explained as the ongoing process of repentance, forgiveness, and renewal in the Christian life. As evidenced in this text, this, too, is something outside of us. It is something that the Holy Spirit continually does for us through God's Word of truth.

26. Sinful humanity is dead in its trespasses and sins. The right relationship between God and humankind was destroyed in the fall. However, God loves fallen human beings despite our sinful rebellion against Him. He is gracious and merciful, and through faith has restored us to Himself and made us alive in Christ. Because of this, Paul says in verse 6 that God raised us up with Christ and places us in the heavenly places.

27. While Ephesians 2:8–9 is often trumpeted by Lutherans, verse 10 makes very clear that God has even more in store for His chosen people. Christians are called to do good works in this world, to serve their neighbor with the love of Christ, and as we will see, to submit to the authorities that God has established for them.

28. All earthly authorities derive their power from the ultimate authority of God, who rules over all things. Therefore, submission to these earthly authorities is also submission to the greater authority of God. These authorities have been established by God to serve us. Whereas Christians are called to be loving and merciful in their inter-

personal relationships, governmental authorities have a God-given mandate to enforce the law and punish evildoers.

There have been corrupt leaders and governmental systems throughout the history of the world, and there always will be. In the words of the Confessions, "It is necessary for Christians to be obedient to their rulers and laws. The only exception is when they are commanded to sin. Then they ought to obey God rather than men (Acts 5:29)" (Augsburg Confession XVI 6–7). In Acts 5:29, when the disciples were forbidden by law to preach the Gospel, they answered, "We must obey God rather than men." Luther believed that when it was necessary to disobey the authorities, Christians should be willing to accept the punishment and face martyrdom rather than obey a godless law. As citizens and Christians, we have the duty to speak out against the murder of unborn children, embryonic stem-cell research, homosexual marriage, and other godless laws or practices.

29. In these two passages, Jesus distinguishes between God's rule through earthly governments, represented at that time and place by Pilate, and God's rule of His kingdom of grace through Christ. In John 18:36, Jesus tells Pilate that His kingdom is not of this world. If God's kingdom were simply an earthly one, then Christians would have no hope! For an earthly king to be humiliated and crucified, as Jesus was, would have been a disgrace. The cross is foolishness to the world, but it means life and salvation for those who believe in Christ. In John 19:9–12, Jesus says Pilate has no authority other than what has been given by God. Truly, Pilate didn't have the power to condemn Jesus to death. As Christ says, "For this reason the Father loves me, because I lay down my life that I may take it up again. No one takes it from me, but I lay it down of my own accord" (John 10:17–18). Jesus laid down His life willingly. Through faith in Him, we have access to His kingdom of heaven on earth so that we will live and reign with Him into everlasting life.

Living in Two Kingdoms (Connect)

30. In the earthly realm, God deals with His whole creation according to His Law. One must work in this world in order to achieve. One must obey earthly authorities (Fourth Commandment). God preserves all people with the blessings of His creation, but this world will fade away. The gifts given here don't last. In the heavenly realm, God operates under the principle of grace according to His Gospel. We do not rely upon our works for citizenship in His kingdom.

Rather, God makes us His own through faith in His Son. God not only preserves the Christian in this life but also provides salvation and eternal life in this never-ending kingdom.

31. Answers may vary. One example might be to say that Christian parents should not punish their children for misbehavior; rather, they should be forgiving and loving, just as God is forgiving and loving. Another confusion of the two kingdoms would be to say that no one in the maximum-security wing at a state prison could possibly be a Christian because they've been convicted of such heinous crimes.

Confusion of the two kingdoms is really a confusion of God's Law and Gospel. In this world, parents should discipline their children because that is the job that God has given them to do. Furthermore, if someone breaks the law of the land, they should be brought to justice through the legal system. However, just because someone has been found guilty in a court of law does not mean that he or she stands guilty before the throne of God. There is a completely different standard in the heavenly kingdom, a standard that does not depend upon one's own works or efforts but upon Christ's alone, which are received through repentant faith. The thief on the cross was rightly punished according to the current law of the land, administered by the Romans. Nevertheless, that day he joined Christ in paradise, even as He promised (Luke 24:39–43).

Will This World Ever Change? (Vision)

32. This world will never change. It hasn't gotten any closer to perfect harmony, and it never will. In fact, one could argue that the world has become even more disconnected than it once was. However, it is important to note that sin is sin, and humankind is no more sinful today than it was in the past. It's just that today, sin in the world goes largely unchecked. Sin will never allow humankind to correct itself or this fallen world.

33. Answers may vary. In this passage, Paul illustrates the many hardships that Christians face in this world of sin but proclaims the greatness of God's eternal glory. Though it may be unseen at the moment, we share in this glory with Christ. As Christians in this world of sin, we fix our eyes upon Christ and the glory promised to us for His sake.

Vocation in the Christian Home

Objectives

By the power of the Holy Spirit working through God's Word, participants will (1) recognize the many vocations that exist within the home, (2) articulate the specific duties for individuals within the Christian home, and (3) examine their responsibilities within the home according to the office God has placed them into.

Opening Worship

O almighty God, whom to know is everlasting life, grant us without all doubt to know Your Son Jesus Christ to be the Way, the Truth, and the Life that, following His steps, we may steadfastly walk in the way that leads to eternal life; through Jesus Christ, our Lord, who lives and reigns with You and the Holy Spirit, one God, now and forever. Amen.

Sing "Oh, Blest the House" (*LSB* 862; *ELH* 190; *CW* 506; *LW* 467; *LBW* 512; *TLH* 625).

Focus

34. Answers may vary. Participants should note that there has been a general decline in Christian and family values in our culture over the last fifty years. This has much to do with the overwhelming disconnect between churches and families today. There are many examples and points of discussion that participants will want to share. Limit the discussion to only a few minutes.

God-Given Roles within the Home (Inform)

35. When God created Adam and Eve, He gave them the divine command to *be fruitful and multiply*. In reading Genesis 2, more detail is given concerning the relationship between the man and the woman. God created the woman to be a suitable helper for the man,

in other words, for *companionship*. When Adam awoke and saw Eve, his wife, he loved her in way that could not be replicated by anything else in God's new creation. It was an intimate, deeply personal love that Adam and Eve had for one another. Furthermore, a man and a woman *complete one another*. Jesus reiterates this truth in Matthew 19:5, "Therefore a man shall leave his father and his mother and hold fast to his wife, and they shall become one flesh."

36. Christians are called to serve their neighbors, and a person's closest neighbors are others within the home. Believers are to submit to one another "out of reverence for Christ" (v. 21). Wives submit to their husbands "as to the Lord" (v. 22), and husbands "love [their] wives, as Christ loved the church" (v. 25), that is, sacrificially. When God defines our roles in marriage, then husbands and wives are freed from worrying about their own needs being met and are protected from the fear that their spouse may seek to dominate.

Participants may be able to share specific struggles and difficulties within marriage. It is important to point out that God's arrangement for marriage is perfect, but as with everything else in this world, sin has corrupted what God created as perfect.

37. In Ephesians 5, the husband, who is the head of the home, is analogous to Christ, who is the head of the Church. Paul compares the wife to the Church, which is the bride of Christ. Therefore, just as the Church submits to Christ, a wife submits to her husband. Likewise, just as Christ offered Himself entirely for the benefit of the Church, so, too, does a husband offer himself sacrificially for the benefit of his wife. God instituted marriage; therefore, husbands and wives have God-given offices with God-given duties. Paul could have used any sort of an analogy he wanted to illustrate the relationship between husband and wife. However, he uses the correlation between our Lord and His Church to show the great significance of the marriage relationship.

38. Encourage participants to answer this question based upon their experience or prior knowledge. Paul emphasizes that a major component of vocation in parenthood is raising children "in the discipline and instruction of the Lord" (Ephesians 6:4).

39. The Fourth Commandment (the first of those dealing with our relationships to one another) is to honor one's father and mother. Children have been called to obey their parents. Another role for children within the home is implicit in Paul's charge to parents— children are to learn from their parents. Not only do children learn

basic social skills in the home, but they also learn the Christian faith there.

At times, raising children can be one of the most frustrating things in the world. But it can also be the most rewarding. God has given both fathers and mothers authority over their children. However, it is important that a parent's duties and authoritative position not be abused. Children need discipline and love. When parents are firm but loving and willing to teach, they will help to shape their children and prepare them for adulthood. A father (or mother) who is overbearing or antagonistic toward his children is not fulfilling the duties that God has given him. A father who continually frustrates his children is not providing for them the environment that God wills for bringing up a child in the faith.

40. Inspired by the Holy Spirit, Solomon proclaims in this psalm that children are a blessing from God. The leader may wish to expand upon this through a discussion with the participants about how children are a blessing.

Solomon is quick to point out the necessary foundation for the home: "Unless the LORD builds the house, those who build it labor in vain" (Psalm 127:1). Answers may vary as to why this is true. The leader may point out that a home established upon the foundation of Christ is built upon an eternal source. A home without a biblical foundation is ultimately empty, because all the material things gathered within it will not last into eternity.

Unfortunately, in the homes of unbelievers, even the relationships that the family members have established with one another will not last. As believers, we have the comfort and joy of knowing that together we make up the body of Christ. The relationships that we have with other believers here on earth, including especially those in the home, will last into eternity.

Treasuring Catechesis (Connect)

41. Answers may vary. Generate discussion and ask any who already use Luther's Small Catechism in the home to share the benefits of doing so. The Small Catechism helps parents teach the faith by giving them a ready-made devotional guide that is based upon the Word of God. Parents themselves will benefit from a continual review of the Small Catechism because their own understanding of the faith will be strengthened.

Luther's carefully crafted words and rhythmic writing will put the faith on the tongue of each child who is exposed to the catechism. The repetition of the text benefits children, encouraging them to learn it by heart. Even though they may not fully understand everything in the Small Catechism, it is better to give children a faith to grow into than a faith to grow out of.

42. Parents have the primary responsibility to instruct their children in the Christian faith. Children should not arrive on the first day of Sunday School, confirmation class, or Lutheran Day School having no familiarity with the Bible, Bible stories, the Small Catechism, Christian hymns, or how to pray. Children need more time in God's Word and instruction in the faith than they can receive outside the home. However, when they attend Sunday School, confirmation class, or Day School, then the teacher or pastor becomes an extension of the parental office.

Distinction between Office and Person (Vision)

43. Answers may vary. However, as most parents will attest, if they are doing their job, their children will not always like them. Children don't like to be disciplined, but parents must discipline their children so that they learn right from wrong. A child can and should honor his or her father and mother, even if he or she thinks they are a little geeky. There is a distinction between the duties that a parent has and the actual person. Whether or not children "like" their parents has little to do with whether or not they should obey them. Parents are entrusted by God with the care of their children. This is the office they hold within the home, and it should be held in the highest regard. It is indeed a great blessing for children both to honor *and* to enjoy their parents, although for many this may not occur until the children reach adulthood.

44. As we read earlier in the lesson, a father's authority is based upon the authority that Christ has given. When James and John came to Jesus requesting places of honor and authority next to Him, Jesus told them that they were not to seek honored positions to lord authority over anyone but were to be servants to all (see Mark 10:35–45). Lead participants in a discussion about how parents can lovingly serve their children while maintaining the authority that God has given them in the home.

Christianity in the Workplace

Objectives

By the power of the Holy Spirit working through God's Word, participants will (1) examine the Christian's vocation in the secular workplace, (2) compare and contrast the work of a Christian to the work of a non-Christian, and (3) recognize effective ways to evangelize in the workplace.

Opening Worship

Merciful and everlasting God, You did not spare Your only Son but delivered Him up for us all that He might bear our sins on the cross. Grant that our hearts may be so fixed with steadfast faith in Him that we may not fear the power of any adversaries; through Jesus Christ, our Lord, who lives and reigns with You and the Holy Spirit, one God, now and forever. Amen.

Sing "Guide Me, O Thou Great Redeemer" (*LSB* 918; *ELH* 262; *CW* 331; *LW* 220; *LBW* 343; *TLH* 54).

Focus

45. Answers may vary. Participants should note that any work benefiting others can be done to the glory of God. However, "jobs" such as dealing drugs, prostitution, or working for organized crime go against God's will and do not uplift humanity. Thus, they cannot be done for the glory of God and should not be done by Christians. Non-Christians, of course, should not serve as Christian pastors or called church workers.

Relationships in the Workplace (Inform)

46. Paul does not say here (or elsewhere in his Epistles) that working under the authority of another is a shameful or degrading position. A Christian should serve his or her master (a vocation that would be the equivalent of today's boss, supervisor, or crew leader) with "fear and trembling" and not for the sake of appearance or to

move up the corporate ladder. Submission in the workplace is submission to Christ. Paul expresses here that a person's earthly master is to be obeyed as one would obey Christ.

47. Participants will draw upon their own experiences to answer this question. Because of our sinful nature, struggles between supervisors and employees are prevalent in nearly every place of work. Paul does not say that a master's authority should be disregarded or becomes invalid when the work environment is harsh or abusive. Ultimately, mistreatment from one's superior does not preclude a Christian from fulfilling his or her duties in that place.

48. Those in supervisory positions have been given the same charge as those in subordinate positions. In addition, they've been given an even greater responsibility. Those in positions of authority give the sinful flesh an opportunity to poke up its ugly head and take advantage of those under their authority. Paul warns those in authority not to be threatening to those under them. Masters are to recognize that the authority they've been given comes from God, who is Lord over all, including themselves *and* those under them. Therefore, a superior office does not give a person license to be disrespectful to others or lord authority over anyone. A person can be in a position of authority and still be a servant to all. When an employer treats his or her employees with respect, that respect is easily reciprocated. This makes the workplace more pleasant and productive.

49. Using the passages cited, assist participants in generating a discussion about what it means that there is no partiality with God. It is important to note that distinctions in office are made for our earthly positions but do not cross over into the heavenly kingdom. Distinctions between our earthly vocations benefit us because without them there would be chaos in the world. But before God, there is not master or slave, supervisor or employee, boss or errand person, for we are all heirs of His heavenly kingdom. There is no partiality with God— He loves us and saves us all the same!

50. This parable illustrates for us that there is no partiality with God. The compensation, so to speak, that we receive in Christ is the same for everyone, no matter who they are or how long they've been a Christian. It is God's grace. Our salvation is based upon the generosity of our heavenly Father and the gifts He bestows in and through Christ.

Even though some of the workers in the parable only worked one hour, they got paid the same amount as those who had worked all day. In our world, this would be an unfair practice that would not be allowed by any labor union. This arrangement works for the kingdom of heaven, however, because our reward is not based upon our own labors but upon the labors of Christ. He holds nothing back. Through His life, death, and resurrection, He has given all things to those who believe in Him.

51. A Christian employer should not adopt the sort of practice illustrated in this parable. Jesus is talking about the kingdom of heaven in Matthew 20, not about how a Christian ought to do things. This model would not work in the world. Because of our sinful nature, people need to be motivated by the Law in order to get up and go to work. If employees know that they will be paid the same no matter what time they show up for work, how inclined would they be to make there on time? While a Christian ought to have a higher work ethic than that, the sinful nature corrupts even the best of intentions.

Working in a Secular Environment (Connect)

52. Answers may vary. Based on the teaching in the "Inform" section, generate practical suggestions for how to deal with some of these challenges. Focus on the distinction between one's place in this world versus one's place in God's kingdom, as well as prayer, worship (see next question), and support from other Christians.

53. Allow participants to share their opinions. Going to church should not become one more item on a long list of things to do each week. Our faith is fed through worship. All week long, we are working to fulfill our vocations in this world, but in worship we receive from Christ a glimpse of our eternal inheritance. Further, we rejoice in the fact that we can rest in His work for us. Worship strengthens us so that we can go out into the world with the assurance of Christ's forgiveness and be equipped for service to our neighbors in the workplace (and elsewhere). Despite the struggles and difficulties in this life, our faith keeps us going and provides hope for us as we look forward to the fullness of the life that awaits us (see Romans 8:18–28).

Worship beyond the Sanctuary (Vision)

54. Through their vocation in the workplace, Christians may have more access to nonbelievers than a pastor does. When Christians and non-Christians work together and get to know each other, friendships, bonds, and trust are often formed, resulting in opportunities to share Christ. Typically, these are friendships that would not have developed otherwise. This is why worship and study of God's

Word is so important, because it is through one's vocation in the workplace that evangelism can happen effectively.

55. Answers may vary. Here are some suggestions: In the workplace, we should adopt the catchphrase of Popeye, "I am what I am!" Our Christianity is a large part of who we are. However, you don't have to talk about your faith all the time or beat people over the head with it. *Be* a Christian, and people will know you *are* a Christian. Do what's expected of you in the workplace, be respectful and obedient to your employer, be courteous and respectful to your co-workers, and don't pilfer your employer's goods or time.

After relationships have been formed with your co-workers, they are more likely to come to you and inquire about your faith. As Peter writes in his Epistle, be prepared to give an answer, don't pursue arguments, and be of service to your co-workers by treating them with the love and respect of Christ.

Freedom of the Christian

Objectives

By the power of the Holy Spirit working through God's Word, participants will (1) understand that it is for freedom that Christ has set us free; (2) realize that good works are necessary, but not necessary for salvation; and (3) discuss ways in which we can exercise Christian freedom appropriately.

Opening Worship

O God, for our redemption You gave Your only Son to suffer death on the cross, and by His glorious resurrection You delivered us from the power of death. Make us die every day to sin so that we may rise to live with Christ forever; who lives and reigns with You and the Holy Spirit, one God, now and forever. Amen.

Sing "Let Us Ever Walk with Jesus" (*LSB* 685; *ELH* 236; *CW* 452; *LW* 381; *LBW* 487; *TLH* 409).

Focus

56. Christian freedom means that we are freed from the condemnation of God's Law. However, we are still bound to keep the civil laws that have been enacted for the sake of good order in the world. The distinction between the two kingdoms helps us understand the paradoxical nature of the Christian life because it distinguishes between God's mode of operation in one kingdom versus the other (earthly kingdom = Law; heavenly kingdom = Gospel).

Slaves unto Righteousness (Inform)

57. Christ has freed us from spiritual slavery and fulfilled for us every obligation to the Law. In this Epistle, Paul is warning the Galatians not to compromise the truth of God's Gospel. If they would agree with those who insisted that Christians must be circumcised in order to be saved, they would once again be placing themselves in bondage. If our place in God's kingdom comes through keeping the

Law, then we are no longer free but slaves to the Law. This is a serious problem because the Gospel cannot be robbed of its sweetness and still be Good News.

58. Even though God no longer counts our sins against us, Paul warns Christians not to indulge the sinful nature. Christians continue to have an obligation to love one another through Christian service, not in order to earn salvation but because salvation has already been given as a gift. Also, sin always has consequences, including the power to tear down and destroy in the temporal realm.

59. A Christian is at the same time sinner and saint. The sinful nature and the Spirit are contrary to one another. There is a constant struggle within the Christian's own person—between the sinful self and the renewed self in Christ. Where the sinful nature seeks after its own pleasures, the new person in Christ seeks to do the will of God.

Because we are in Christ, our sins no longer have the power to separate us from God. He cleanses us. But we still struggle with the sinfulness of our flesh, which seeks ways to abuse the freedom that we've been given in Christ. In selfish sinfulness, we take advantage of God's grace and neglect the needs of others.

60. Even though we have many freedoms in Christ, there may be certain times when the exercise of those freedoms wouldn't be appropriate. Not everything is beneficial, and exercising one's freedom could cause offense to a Christian with weaker faith. We may have a full understanding of what our freedom in Christ means, but others may not. If our demonstration of Christian freedom causes others to sin or to question their own faith, it would be best to refrain from such an action.

The difference between this admonition and Paul's warning to the Church in Galatia is that of motivation. Out of Christian love, a person might choose not to exercise Christian freedom because he or she is free to do it and free not to do it. It is truly a matter of freedom and choice. However, it would not have been a matter of Christian freedom for the Galatians to succumb to the circumcision group because it was a serious violation against an article of faith. In a situation such as this, it is important for the sake of the Gospel not to compromise, give in, or allow others to make legalistic demands that can potentially damage faith.

61. Just as Paul says, "When you were slaves of sin, you were free in regard to righteousness" (Romans 6:20), the reciprocal is also true. When you are slaves to righteousness, you are freed from the control of sin! Once Christ cleanses you of your sinfulness, He also

makes you righteous. Therefore, becoming a slave to righteousness is the natural consequence of being freed from sin.

The designation of "slave to sin" or "slave to righteousness" comes as a result of who your master is. If your master is sin, you are a slave to sin. If your master is Christ, you are a slave to righteousness. Jesus says, "No one can serve two masters, for either he will hate the one and love the other, or he will be devoted to the one and despise the other. You cannot serve God and money" (Matthew 6:24).

62. Our lives in Christ are defined by our master. We have been given a new status—slaves to righteousness. As such, serving others with the love of Christ is simply what we do according to our new nature in Christ. This gives vocation its Gospel character.

Freed to Serve (Connect)

63. Not only have we been freed from sin, which ensures our eternal salvation, but we have been freed to do good works. Before our union with Christ, our sinful nature defined who we were and what we did. Since our master was the sinful flesh, we were enslaved to sin, unable to do anything good in the eyes of God. As Jesus explains to Peter in Matthew 18, since we have been freed from such a huge debt, we've been given the ability and the responsibility to forgive those minor debts our neighbor owes us.

64. The ultimate goal of evangelism is to tell the Good News of Christ's *forgiveness*. Christianity would be no different than any other world religion if it were based upon human works. Although our sinful pride may enjoy trying to keep the Law, thus earning our righteousness, this is not comforting at all. When we become` aware of sin (through the Law), there is only one way to be relieved from that burden. The Gospel tells us of Christ's salvation, which is a free gift, with no strings attached.

The Reality of Sin (Vision)

65. Answers may vary. These struggles trouble us because as redeemed children of Christ, we don't want to sin against God or against our neighbor. As Christians, we agree that the Law is good, as Paul explains in Romans 7, and so we desire to follow it. In our struggle with sin, we cry out with Paul, "Wretched man that I am! Who will deliver me from this body of death? Thanks be to God through Jesus Christ our Lord!" (vv. 24–25)

66. There will always be struggle in the Christian life. Even though this is troubling for us, the struggles between the old self and the new self are evidence that our faith is alive. It is evidence that the Holy Spirit is working in our lives, convicting us of our sins and driving us to repentance. These struggles shouldn't concern us in regard to our salvation; we should never think that they come as a result of our lack of faith.

Since we will never reach a point in our earthly lives when we no longer struggle against the sinfulness of our flesh, it would be very alarming indeed if we were to become so complacent in our sin that we aren't at all troubled by it. If we were to think we could go on sinning without any regard for God's Law, this would be evidence that faith is dead. We have a continual need to confess our sins before God our Father and receive the forgiveness that Christ freely offers.

Because we are in Christ, we are no longer condemned (Romans 8:1). Our connection to Christ through faith—brought about through the Gospel and the Sacraments—is the means by which we receive the forgiveness of sins that Christ won for us on the cross. Christ is our only hope and source of good works, just as He is our only hope and source of the forgiveness of sins and eternal life. To God alone be all praise and glory!

Appendix of Lutheran Teaching

Below you will find examples of how the first Lutherans addressed the issue of vocation. They will help you understand this important aspect of Lutheran spirituality.

Augsburg Confession

Our churches teach that this faith is bound to bring forth good fruit (Galatians 5:22–23). It is necessary to do good works commanded by God (Ephesians 2:10), because of God's will. We should not rely on those works to merit justification before God. The forgiveness of sins and justification is received through faith. The voice of Christ testifies, "So you also, when you have done all that you were commanded, say, 'We are unworthy servants; we have only done what was our duty'" (Luke 17:10). The Fathers teach the same thing. Ambrose says, "It is ordained of God that he who believes in Christ is saved, freely receiving forgiveness of sins, without works, through faith alone." (VI 1–3)

Our churches teach that lawful civil regulations are good works of God. They teach that it is right for Christians to hold political office, to serve as judges, to judge matters by Imperial laws and other existing laws, to impose just punishments, to engage in just wars, to serve as soldiers, to make legal contracts, to hold property, to take oaths when required by the magistrates, for a man to marry a wife, or a woman to be given in marriage (Romans 13; 1 Corinthians 7:2). (XVI 1–2)

This is why our teachers teach the churches about faith in this way.

First, they teach that our works cannot reconcile God to us or merit forgiveness of sins, grace, and justification. We obtain reconciliation only by faith when we believe that we are received into favor for Christ's sake. He alone has been set forth as the Mediator and Atoning Sacrifice (1 Timothy 2:5), in order that the Father may be reconciled through Him. Therefore, whoever believes that he merits grace by works despises the merit and grace of Christ (Galatians 5:4). In so doing, he is seeking a way to God without Christ, by human strength, although Christ Himself said, "I am the way, and the truth, and the life" (John 14:6). . . .

Furthermore, we teach that it is necessary to do good works. This does not mean that we merit grace by doing good works, but because it is God's will (Ephesians 2:10). It is only by faith, and nothing else, that forgiveness of sins is apprehended. The Holy Spirit is received through faith, hearts are renewed and given new affections, and then they are able to bring forth good works. Ambrose says: "Faith is the mother of a good will and doing what is right." (XX 8–10, 27–30)

Apology of the Augsburg Confession

This entire topic *about the distinction between the spiritual kingdom of Christ and a political kingdom* has been explained in the literature of our writers. Christ's kingdom is spiritual (John 18:36). This means that the knowledge of God, the fear of God and faith, eternal righteousness, and eternal life begin in the heart. Meanwhile, Christ's kingdom allows us outwardly to use legitimate political ordinances of every nation in which we live, just as it allows us to use medicine or the art of building, or food, drink, and air. Neither does the Gospel offer new laws about the public state, but commands that we obey present laws, whether they have been framed by heathens or by others. It commands that in this obedience we should exercise love. (XVI 54–55)

For Christ's Church always held that the forgiveness of sins is received freely. Indeed, the Pelagians were condemned. They argued that grace is given because of our works. Besides, we have shown above well enough that we hold that good works should follow faith. "Do we then overthrow the law?" asks Paul. "On the contrary, we uphold the law" (Romans 3:31), because when we have received the Holy Spirit through faith, the fulfilling of the Law necessarily follows. Patience, chastity, and other fruit of the Spirit gradually grow by this love. (XX 91–92)

Smalcald Articles

I do not know how to change in the least what I have previously and constantly taught about justification. Namely, that through faith, as St. Peter says, we have a new and clean heart (Acts 15:9–11), and

God will and does account us entirely righteous and holy for the sake of Christ, our Mediator (1 Timothy 2:5). Although sin in the flesh has not yet been completely removed or become dead (Romans 7:18), yet He will not punish or remember it.

Such faith, renewal, and forgiveness of sins are followed by good works (Ephesians 2:8–9). What is still sinful or imperfect in them will not be counted as sin or defect, for Christ's sake (Psalm 32:1–2; Romans 4:7–8). The entire individual, both his person and his works, is declared to be righteous and holy from pure grace and mercy, shed upon us and spread over us in Christ. Therefore, we cannot boast of many merits and works, if they are viewed apart from grace and mercy. As it is written, "Let the one who boasts, boast in the Lord" (1 Corinthians 1:31); namely, that he has a gracious God. For with that, all is well. We say, besides, that if good works do not follow, the faith is false and not true. (XIII 1–4)

Formula of Concord
AFFIRMATIVE STATEMENTS

The Pure Teaching of the Christian Churches about This Controversy

For the thorough statement and decision of this controversy, our doctrine, faith, and confession is as follows:

1. Good works certainly and without doubt follow true faith—if it is not a dead, but a living faith—just as fruit grows on a good tree (Matthew 7:17).

2. We believe, teach, and confess that good works should be entirely excluded from the question about salvation, just as they are excluded from the article of justification before God. The apostle testifies with clear words when he writes as follows, "Just as David also speaks of the blessing of the one to whom God counts righteousness apart from works: . . . 'Blessed is the man against whom the Lord will not count his sin'" (Romans 4:6–8). And again, "For by grace you have been saved through faith. And this is not your own doing; it is the gift of God, not a result of works, so that no one may boast" (Ephesians 2:8–9).

3. We also believe, teach, and confess that all people, but especially those who are born again and renewed by the Holy Spirit, are obligated to do good works (Ephesians 2:10).

4. In this sense the words *necessary*, *shall*, and *must* are used correctly and in a Christian way to describe the regenerate, and are in no way contrary to the form of sound words and speech.

5. Nevertheless, if the words mentioned (i.e., *necessity* and *necessary*) are used when talking about regenerate people, then only due obedience—not coercion—is to be understood. For the truly believing, so far as they are regenerate, do not offer obedience from coercion or the driving of the Law, but from a voluntary spirit. For they are no more under the Law, but under grace (Romans 6:14; 7:6; 8:14).

6. We also believe, teach, and confess that when it is said, "The regenerate do good works from a free spirit," this is not to be understood as though it were an option for the regenerate person to do or not to do good when he wants, as though a person can still retain faith if he intentionally perseveres in sins (1 John 2:5–9).

7. This is not to be understood in any other way than as the Lord Christ and His apostles themselves declare. In other words, the free spirit does not obey from fear of punishment, like a servant, but from love of righteousness, like children (Romans 8:15).

8. However, this willingness in God's elect children is not perfect. It is burdened with great weakness, as St. Paul complains about himself in Romans 7:14–25 and Galatians 5:17.

9. Nevertheless, for the sake of the Lord Christ, the Lord does not charge this weakness to His elect, as it is written, "There is therefore now no condemnation for those who are in Christ Jesus" (Romans 8:1).

10. We believe, teach, and confess also that works do not maintain faith and salvation in us, but God's Spirit alone does this, through faith. Good works are evidences of His presence and indwelling (Romans 8:5, 14). (Epitome IV 5–15)

Glossary

Anfechtung. This word was used by Luther to describe the relentless attack of the devil on the conscience, as the old evil foe uses the Law in an effort to tempt Christians to unbelief and despair. There is no solution for *Anfechtung* other than Absolution, which promises Christ's victory in weakness and defeat.

antinomianism. The teaching that the Law has no place in Christian proclamation or in the life of the believer. This view was championed by John Agricola at the time of the Reformation. It was rejected by both Luther and the Lutheran Confessions as it ultimately turned the Gospel into a new law.

cafeterianism. An attempt to create one's own worldview by selecting, cafeteria-style, religious or moral concepts, ideas, and practices from a variety of sources. A person who attends a Christian church on Sunday while believing in reincarnation might be viewed as a "cafeterian," for example, since bodily resurrection and reincarnation are inherently incompatible.

confession. Literally, to say the same thing that God says. When we confess our sins, we repeat God's evaluation of our sin.

contrition. The sorrow over sin that is created by God's Law as it breaks the heart held captive by sin. Contrition is not a self-generated regret; rather, it is the work done by the Spirit as He convicts a person of sin.

coram Deo. Before God.

Deus absconditus. The hidden God, or God as He hides Himself.

Deus revelatus. The revealed God, or God as He reveals Himself in Christ.

efficacy of the Word. The power of God's Word to effect or accomplish its divine purpose.

enthusiasts. A term used by Luther to refer to the radical spiritualists who believed that God came to them apart from the external instruments of Word and Sacrament.

extra nos. Outside of us. Used to refer to the external character of the Gospel and Sacraments.

forensic justification. God renders a verdict that declares the unrighteous person righteous for the sake of Jesus' atoning work on the cross.

humanism. A broad range of philosophies that emphasize human dignity and worth and recognize a common morality based on universal, rational human nature. Humanists who deny the possibility of any supernatural involvement in human affairs are sometimes called *secular* humanists.

larvae Dei. Literally, the "masks" God wears to serve us. Through vocation, or calling, God serves us while concealing Himself behind the masks of our spouse, employer, family member, public servant, or neighbor.

mysticism. While mysticism itself is a broad form of spirituality with distinct nuances, it is best characterized by the movement to transcend or move above the earthly through inward experience.

Office of the Keys. The authority that Christ has given His Church to "unlock" from their sins those who repent and to "lock" those who refuse to repent to their sins.

opinio legis. The "opinion of the Law" that God deals with us on the basis of our works, which must account for something in the scheme of salvation.

penance. In Roman Catholic theology, the third sacrament, consisting of three parts: contrition, confession to the priest, and works of satisfaction.

Pietism. A post-Reformation religious movement associated with Philip Spener (1635–1705) that was characterized by a shift from the objective reality of Christ's gifts to the subjective appropriation of the Gospel and the subsequent renewal of the believer's life personally and socially.

postmodernism. Refers to a cluster of themes that are somewhat interconnected in their opposition to the attempts to establish truthfulness, which characterized the period of modernity. The focus of postmodernism is characterized by pluralism and the rejection of claims to absolute truth.

oratio, meditatio, tentatio. Prayer, meditation, and trial. Luther said that theologians (students of God's Word) are made by prayer, meditation, and the trial of life under the cross.

Rationalism. The Enlightenment movement that saw human reason as the ultimate criterion for reality.

revelation. God's act of making His will manifest in both Law and Gospel to human beings. The instrument of God's revelation is the prophetic and apostolic Scriptures.

theology of glory. A theology of mystic and scholastic speculation, which holds that true knowledge of God derives from the study of nature, which reflects God's glory. A theology of glory focuses on human reason, mysticism, or morality.

theology of the cross. A term gleaned from Luther's Heidelberg Disputation of 1518, referring to a theology that is derived from the study of the humiliation, sufferings, and death of Christ.